# CELEBRATE YOUR PERIOD

## THE ULTIMATE PUBERTY BOOK for PRETEEN and TEEN GIRLS

**AMANDA D'ALMEIDA**

**Illustrated by CAIT BRENNAN**

**ROCKRIDGE PRESS**

For general information on our other products and services or to obtain technical support, please contact our Customer Care Department within the United States at (866) 744-2665, or outside the United States at (510) 253-0500.

Rockridge Press publishes its books in a variety of electronic and print formats. Some content that appears in print may not be available in electronic books, and vice versa.

Interior and Cover Designer: Jill Lee
Art Producer: Alyssa Williams
Editor: Jeanann Pannasch
Production Editor: Nora Milman
Production Manager: Martin Worthington

Illustration © 2022 Cait Brennan

Paperback ISBN: 978-1-63878-388-6 | eBook ISBN: 978-1-63878-555-2
R0

# CELEBRATE YOUR PERIOD

For those who are going through changes and seeking out answers. Hopefully, this book empowers you to go through this exciting time of growth with strength and confidence.

# CONTENTS

# INTRODUCTION

| | | | | | | | | | | | | | | | | | | | | | | | | | | | | | | | | | | | |

**Welcome** to a celebration of you and your amazing
body! I am thrilled you're here to join me in this journey
of exploring everything about menstruation, more commonly known as periods. You're probably here because
you started or are just about to start your period. You
may have already noticed some changes in your body
and emotions. Starting menstruation is an exciting and
big change. In this book, I'll give you knowledge about
this time of your life so you can navigate through your
period and changing body with confidence!

I'm passionate about talking about puberty, periods, and women's health. I am going to graduate as a medical doctor in a couple of months! I also cofounded Medicine Explained, a health education platform with more than 1.7 million followers and over 550 million views on our hashtag #medicineexplained. My partner and I have created many explainers about puberty, periods, and overall health. I get a lot of questions every day about periods and puberty. There probably isn't a question that you have about your body that we haven't been asked! In this book, I'll answer some of the most common and important questions you may have. Don't worry if you feel like you know absolutely nothing about periods. We aren't born with this information, and we all have to learn it somewhere. Before we get into the nitty-gritty about periods, let's take a second to appreciate how extraordinary your body is, and nothing during this time will change that!

Knowledge is power. When you know what's going on with your body, you can make decisions that are best for your health and avoid being surprised by changes in your body. You know when a friend or sibling hides behind a corner and jumps out to scare you? Your heart beats faster, and you might even yelp. But if you know that person is hiding behind the corner, they aren't able to scare you. I'm giving you information in this book to know what's behind the next corner so you won't be surprised. Not only will this book help you understand menstruation, but it will also give you the confidence, tools, and language to ask a trusted adult for help or advice about your period.

While you will experience many changes in your body, something that will never change is how amazing you are. You are beautiful, strong, and confident. This book will give you the knowledge to stay confident and comfortable and love your body with all the changes you will go through during puberty and with your period.

So what can you expect in this book? Chapter 1 talks about what menstruation is and defines the body parts and hormones involved in this process. We'll talk about some of the incredible biology behind what's going on during your period. This chapter will give you a good foundation to understand the rest of the book. What you can expect from your period, like physical and emotional changes, is covered in chapter 2. Chapter 3 talks about loving your body and ways to track your period. This chapter also explains all the period products that are available and how to use them. Chapter 4 will give you some tools for feeling great through the entire month and living your best and healthiest life. In chapter 5, we'll celebrate you and your awesome work reading this book and taking the time to learn about yourself and your changing body. You'll get a few more tips for learning more, including how to chat with trusted adults and friends about your period. A glossary at the end of the book provides a quick reference for some of the important terms and how to pronounce them. Some words are pretty scientific and may take some time to remember. But it's good knowledge, so have patience and keep learning all you can.

Menstruation is a huge change and an important part of growing up. It's a powerful time, and when you have the knowledge about what you will experience, you'll be able to go through this change with confidence, strength, and pure amazement at what your body is doing. I'm so happy you picked up this book to learn more about your changing body, and I can't wait to help you navigate this journey.

Let's get this party started!

T0016514

# CHAPTER 1

# MY AMAZING, MENSTRUATING BODY

Our bodies change a *lot* as we go through puberty. You'll experience things like your breasts growing, getting taller, starting your period, and more! During puberty, in addition to your body changing, you'll also experience changes in emotions. You may notice new emotions or frequent changes in your moods, which can sometimes feel like a roller coaster with quickly shifting turns.

This book will give you tools to help you navigate puberty and answer questions you may have about your body, your emotions, and your relationships. Throughout your transition into adulthood, there's one thing that won't change: the fact that you are a marvelous human. You are strong and capable. You are powerful enough to handle any change that your body or life throws your way.

# CONNECTING THE DOTS: PUBERTY AND MENSTRUATION

Small and large changes happen during puberty. A simple way to think about puberty is your body transitioning from looking like a child's body to looking like an adult's body. During puberty, as you experience both physical and emotional changes, it's okay to have a bunch of different emotions about this change in your life—that's normal.

One of the biggest changes you will experience during puberty is the start of menstruation, or getting your first period. Simply said, your period is the bleeding phase of the menstrual cycle. Whether you have or haven't started your period yet, or experienced some of the other bodily changes caused by puberty, don't worry. The following pages will provide valuable information to help you explore these changes with confidence. We're going to go through what changes you may notice about your body even before your first period so you have an idea of what to expect when you get it. Let's read on, so you can face your period with strength, excitement, and amazement!

# What to Expect Before Your Period

Getting your period doesn't happen out of nowhere. You'll probably notice other smaller changes in your body that signal, "Hey, we may start our first period soon!" These changes, called "secondary sex characteristics," are outlined in the following section. These developments may feel confusing at first, so I've explained them for you. This way, you can know what to expect and how to prepare for this exciting time of your life.

**BREAST BUD DEVELOPMENT:** One of the first things you may notice when you start puberty is breast bud development. Breasts may grow a bit unevenly. Sometimes breast size evens out, and sometimes it doesn't. Most women have slightly uneven breasts. This is normal. You may get some soreness under your nipples as they grow—this is also normal.

**BODY SHAPE CHANGES:** Your body may change in other ways during puberty. Sometimes the distribution of fat around your body will change. For example, you may develop bigger hips. Whatever size and shape you are, it's important to remember how amazing your body is. Everyone is unique, and our bodies look and develop differently. How cool is that? Loving your own unique body is so important because nobody has one just like yours!

**GROWTH SPURTS:** You may notice that you've grown a couple of inches in a short period of time. Females usually go through puberty before males, so you may notice that you are taller than others in your class. Menstruation usually starts around six months to a year after your biggest growth spurt, but this differs from person to person.

**SKIN CHANGES:** Hormones are a big part of puberty. They are circulating throughout your body, and during puberty, the levels change and go up and down. With changing hormones, you may notice changes in your skin. Some people get pimples or acne. Acne can start at the beginning of puberty and last through the teen or adolescent years. Significant acne usually clears up after your teens years, but it's not uncommon to break-out or to have an occasional pimple when you're older.

**CERVICAL FLUID:** One change that can be surprising is noticing white mucous-like streaks or fluid on your underwear. This is totally normal. It's called cervical fluid or discharge. This may appear about six months before your first period. This is not your period, but it is part of the menstrual cycle. It's just another thing that happens with changing hormones. The cervical fluid can also change in amount, consistency, and appearance throughout the month.

**NEW HAIR GROWTH:** During puberty, you will start to grow hair under your armpits and develop pubic hair, which is hair on and around your genitals. You usually start to grow pubic hair shortly after your breast buds start developing. If your pubic hair starts growing before your breasts, this is also normal. At first, you may notice only a few hairs, but as puberty goes on, the hair will start to fill in. Your leg hair may get darker. Some people choose to shave, but hair is natural. It's not necessary to shave. Many women choose not to shave. Do whatever is most comfortable for you!

# WHAT'S MENSTRUATION ALL ABOUT?

Getting your first period, or menstruating, can be an exciting and sometimes nerve-racking time of life. Your first period is called menarche. Whether you have or haven't started your period, the next few chapters will help guide you through the experience.

Having a period is an important part of puberty and the transition into adulthood. It's also a sign of being fertile. Fertility means that your body is capable of reproducing, or having a baby. Later in life, you may or may not choose to have a baby. That's completely your choice!

Having a period isn't just a sign of fertility—it's also a great sign of overall health. When your hormones are healthy and in balance and you're eating well, you will typically have regular periods (though it's not uncommon to have some irregularity in the first couple of years). Of course, you want to be sure not to compare yourself to others. Everyone's menstrual cycle is different. We'll talk more about that in the next few chapters.

Finally, it's okay to be nervous about getting your first period. Most of us have questions about it. I know I did! This next section will answer some of your questions and give you the knowledge to feel prepared and confident!

## WHEN WILL I GET MY PERIOD?

I get this question a lot. First periods usually occur between the ages of 10 and 15, but the average age is 12. When you get your first period depends on a bunch of different things. Some factors are out of your control, like genetics, when your biological mom went through menarche (the first period), or when Mother Nature decides it's time. If you're experiencing a lot of stress, it can delay menarche. Some medications may also change menarche.

What if you haven't gotten your period? There are many possible reasons for this, which we'll discuss later. If you haven't gotten your period by age 15, it's best to talk to a doctor. Just remember, everyone experiences periods differently!

## LEARNING AND LOVING *YOU*

Now that we've chatted a bit about the changes you can expect during puberty, let's go into the details of some of the anatomy (the structure of the body) and physiology (how the different body parts function). This science is awesome! I continue to be amazed at what our bodies do, but I also love to explore the "why" behind it all. This information can help you better understand your body. Don't worry if you don't understand everything at first—it's a complex system. We are all learning more about how our bodies work every day. You can always come back and refer to this information later.

# The Invisible Bits

We've talked about some of the changes you'll see on the outside, but what's going on underneath our skin, in the places we can't see? Let's define some menstrual cycle terms so you understand them when you see them throughout the book. We'll start with hormones, since they are central to the menstrual cycle.

**HORMONES:** These are chemicals that the body releases naturally. They act like messages being sent throughout the body, telling certain organs what to do. The five hormones listed here—known as the sex hormones—work together to create the menstrual cycle. You may have heard of the first three hormones, since they are more commonly referenced when we talk about changes during puberty or our periods.

- **ESTROGEN:** Estrogen is a hormone mostly produced by the ovaries. It helps regulate the menstrual cycle and develop secondary sex char-acteristics, like breast buds, new hair growth, and cervical fluid. Fun fact: Estrogen also helps protect the brain!

- **PROGESTERONE:** Progesterone is another import-ant hormone for the menstrual cycle and the development of secondary sex characteristics. Progesterone prepares the uterus for pregnancy by protecting the uterine lining as it develops and triggering the lining to get thicker to support an egg.

- **TESTOSTERONE:** Testosterone is the hormone you'll usually hear about when talking about boys, but it's actually really important in your puberty, too! It's crucial for breast development and overall menstrual health. Testosterone can also be converted into estrogen.

- **FOLLICLE-STIMULATING HORMONE (FSH):** This is released by the pituitary gland in the brain. It signals to the ovaries for one of the follicles to grow and mature. The follicle has an egg inside it.

- **LUTEINIZING HORMONE (LH):** This hormone is also released from the pituitary gland in the brain. The "LH surge"—when LH levels get really high—signals to the ovaries for the release of the egg from the follicle and ovary.

**CERVIX (*SUR·VIHKS*):** The cervix connects the vagina and the uterus.

**CORPUS LUTEUM (*KOR·PUHS LOO·TEE·UHM*):** This is like a command center that develops in the ovary. The corpus luteum develops from the follicle after the egg is released. It's pretty much the last stage of the follicle's life. The corpus luteum keeps sending directions as hormones until it gets a signal that the egg is not fertilized.

**ENDOMETRIUM (*EN·DOH·MEE·TREE·UHM*):** This is the tissue that lines the inside of the uterus. It gets

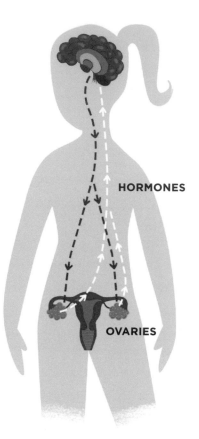

HORMONES

OVARIES

thicker during the menstrual cycle, when the body is preparing for the egg during ovulation, and sheds during menstruation.

**FALLOPIAN TUBES (*FUH·LOW·PEE·UHN TOOBZ*):** These are the tubes that carry an egg from the ovaries to the uterus.

**FOLLICLES (*FAH·LUH·KUHLZ*):** These are sacs in the ovaries that have eggs or ova inside them. One follicle per menstrual cycle is chosen to grow and mature.

**MYOMETRIUM (*MAI·OH·MEE·TREE·UHM*):** Underneath the endometrium is the myometrium. *Myo* = "muscle." It's the muscular part of the uterus. Unlike the endometrium, the myometrium doesn't grow and shed during the menstrual cycle.

**OVA:** Also referred to as "eggs," these are unfertilized cells stored in the ovaries.

**OVARY/OVARIES (*OH·VUH·REE/OH·VUH·REEZ*):** The body has two ovaries where eggs are stored. During the menstrual cycle, this is where the ovum (egg) develops and releases from. Fun fact: We are born with all the eggs we will ever have! One matures each month and is sent from the ovary, down the fallopian tube, to the uterus.

**OVULATION (*AH·VYOO·LAY·SHUHN*):** This is the stage of the menstrual cycle when an egg is released from the ovary into the fallopian tube.

**UTERUS (*YOO·TUHR·UHS*):** This is a hollow organ in the lower abdomen; also called the "womb" since a fertilized egg would implant here during pregnancy.

**VAGINA (*VUH·JAI·NUH*):** The vagina is the muscular tube that connects the cervix to the outer world. This is where a tampon goes if you choose to use one during your periods.

**VULVA (*VUHL·VUH*):** This is the outer genitalia in the pubic area—the parts you can see. It is made up of many specific parts but is generally referred to as the vulva.

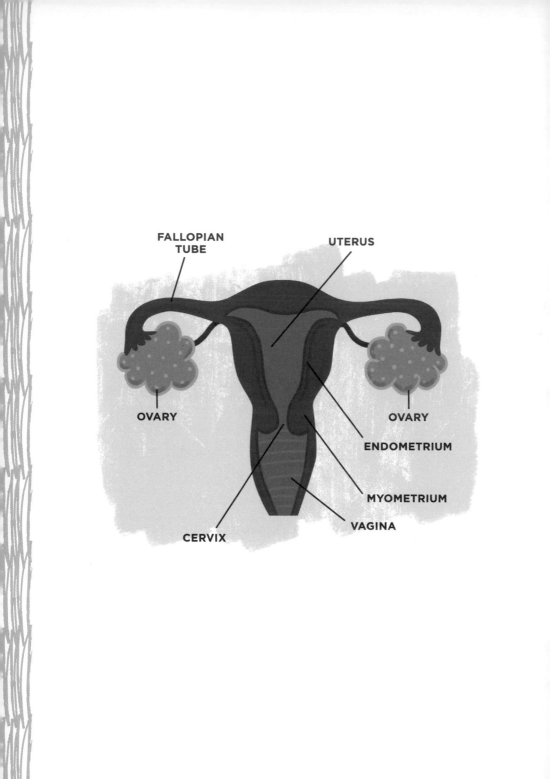

FALLOPIAN
TUBE

UTERUS

OVARY

OVARY

ENDOMETRIUM

MYOMETRIUM

CERVIX

VAGINA

# Working Together

Nice work—you've learned about most of the key play-ers in your menstrual cycle. Now let's talk about how your body parts all work together to make the men-strual cycle happen. Don't worry if you have to read this a couple of times to understand the delicate dance that all of these invisible bits take part in.

Even though everything is connected in a cycle, we will start with the brain. The pituitary gland is the part of the brain that produces hormones that are released into the bloodstream. The follicle-stimulating hormone (FSH) is a hormone that tells the ovaries to prepare an egg for ovulation. Just like its name, it stimulates the follicles to develop. Follicles are sacs with an egg inside. The brain is sending a text via the FSH saying, "Hey ovaries, it's time for some of your eggs to mature and develop!" As the eggs start to mature in the ovaries, the follicles that include the eggs produce estrogen, another hormone.

During each menstrual cycle, multiple eggs and folli-cles develop and mature at the same time. But only one lucky follicle gets chosen to release its egg each men-strual cycle. This egg gets released from the ovary into the fallopian tube and moves along the fallopian tube into the uterus. The release of the egg from the ovary is called ovulation.

The levels of estrogen and progesterone change throughout the cycle. The highest level of estrogen produced by the follicle is right before ovulation. At the same time that the follicle is maturing and growing in the ovary, the uterus is also working by getting signals to grow. The signals are from the estrogen being made by the follicle in the ovary. The uterus is preparing for ovulation, so the endometrium, or lining of the uterus, grows and thickens to make a comfortable spot for the egg to land if it were to be fertilized and potentially become a baby. This place would be cushy and have a bunch of nutrients for the egg to implant and grow.

Then ovulation happens about 13 to 15 days after the start of the last period. The high estrogen levels produced by the follicle right before ovulation signal to the brain to increase another hormone—this one is called luteinizing hormone (LH), which comes from the brain and tells your ovaries to ovulate.

After ovulation, the egg has been released from the follicle, but the rest of the follicle still lives in the ovary. This is called the corpus luteum, and it produces estrogen *and* progesterone. The progesterone protects the lining of the uterus. If the egg is not fertilized, the corpus luteum realizes there is no fertilized egg to support and stops producing the hormones. When the endometrium is no longer protected and supported by estrogen and progesterone (because these levels drop), the endometrium breaks down and sheds—this is what comes out during your period. This bleeding usually happens about 14 days after ovulation. The menstrual cycle starts again the day you start bleeding. As you

can see from all of this, hormone levels change throughout your menstrual cycle—these differences are what
can cause mood changes and physical changes.

Phew! Really good work making it through the physiology of what's going on in your body during your
menstrual period. You've already learned so much—this
will get rid of some of the mystery, hopefully allowing
you to feel powerful and confident as you start
your period.

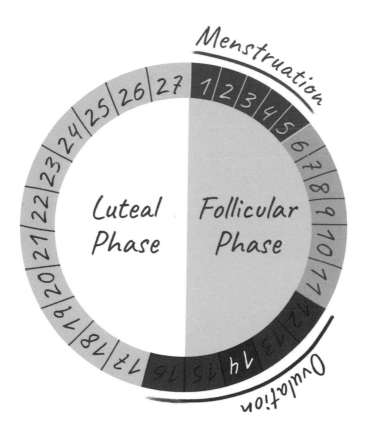

# The Menstrual Cycle

You now know quite a bit about the hormones and organs involved in the menstrual cycle. Awesome job! Now let's talk about the timing of it all. *Menstruation* refers to your period. The menstrual *cycle* is different—it includes both menstruation and the time in between each period. Each menstrual cycle lasts about 28 days. When you first get your period, your cycle may be shorter or longer. Your period should start to get on a regular schedule within a couple of years. When counting the 28 days, the clock starts on the first day that you see blood on your period. These 28 days are broken down into four stages:

- The bleeding phase

- The follicular phase

- The ovulatory phase

- The luteal phase

Phase 1 is the *bleeding phase,* or what we call your "period." The bleeding phase usually lasts three to seven days. Your estrogen and progesterone are at their lowest levels. Getting rid of the body's endometrium tissue takes some energy—so you may feel tired and experience more emotions. You may also feel breast tenderness or cramps.

Phase 2 is the *follicular phase*—this is when the follicle takes the stage. This phase can last from about

10 to 22 days. The bleeding phase is actually part of the follicular phase, so day 1 of the follicular phase and bleeding phase are the same. The pituitary gland in your brain sends messages to the ovaries, choosing one follicle in the ovaries to mature. During this phase, the follicle starts to make estrogen, which thickens the lining of the uterus.

Phase 3 is the *ovulatory phase*. When LH levels get really high, the ovaries get the message to release the egg that has been developing in the chosen follicle. The egg gets released into the fallopian tube and travels into the uterus. During ovulation, you may notice a thicker discharge of cervical fluid in your underwear. The ovulation phase usually happens right in the middle of your cycle, around day 14. The phase lasts about 24 hours.

Phase 4 is the *luteal phase*. This is when the corpus luteum—that follicle that had the egg—is one of the star players. The corpus luteum stays in the ovary after releasing the egg and keeps producing mostly progesterone and some estrogen. When your body realizes the egg was not fertilized, the corpus luteum shrinks, stops producing hormones, and is reabsorbed into your body. The low levels of these hormones signal the bleeding phase to start. Then you start all over again at phase 1! The luteal phase usually lasts around 14 days. This is when you might experience premenstrual syndrome (PMS). We'll talk about symptoms of PMS later.

Now that you know all of this, it's helpful to track your periods to know when you go through each phase. Because hormones are always changing, you may experience different energy levels, emotions, or cravings during the different phases. If you're aware of the changes you may feel in your physical body and emotionally, you're better prepared to care for your body with awareness and understanding.

In the next chapter, we'll explore what you can expect from your period. You'll be able to use this knowledge as a powerful tool to confidently go through your period!

## SHARE SESSIONS

Everyone has a unique and beautiful body. Talking about your period with trusted adults and friends in your life is a great way to learn from their experiences, too. It's interesting and exciting to learn more about other bodies and period experiences. The more we chat about periods, the more *normal* it feels to talk about them. Each conversation about menstruation offers new opportunities to learn and share information with friends. When you do have these period conversations, make sure you don't compare yourself to others—that is, don't be nervous if your period experience isn't like your friends' experiences. You are one of a kind, and so is your period journey!

# CHAPTER 2

# MENSTRUATION EXPECTATIONS

· · · · · · · · · · · · · · · · · · · · · · · · · · · · · · · ·

Amazing! You've learned so much about your body and how periods work. Now we're going to chat about what you may feel physically and emotionally during your menstrual cycle. When it comes to periods, there are a lot of different "normals." If your menstrual cycle doesn't exactly match your friends', that's totally fine. You can learn from other people's period stories, but there's no need to compare yourself to them. We all have unique bodies that work in their own ways.

# WHAT WILL MY PERIOD FEEL LIKE?

Your period will bring many changes, both physical and emotional. We call this *pre*menstrual syndrome or PMS because it happens before (*pre*) your menstrual cycle. PMS is when you feel physical or emotional symptoms a few days before and during your period. If these symptoms happen almost every month, they are referred to as PMS. Official PMS is having emotional or physical symptoms five days before your period and four days after your period begins for three menstrual cycles in a row.

You may have these symptoms during your menstrual cycle anyway, even without the official PMS diagnosis. If you have some of these symptoms, they shouldn't last the whole month. When you first get your period, these symptoms may be a little worse. Some symptoms can get better in a couple of years, and some may stick around. The important thing to know is that you can relieve many of these symptoms. Stay tuned—in chapter 4, I'll give you some tips and tricks for relief.

PMS symptoms are really common, but at times, they could also be your body's signal that you aren't the healthiest you can be. We'll talk about ways you can improve PMS symptoms a little later in chapter 4. If you have PMS, you're not alone. You're also powerful and able to handle these changes! Let's talk about them.

# The Physical Symptoms

**ACNE:** When hormone levels are low, glands in your skin may make more of an oily substance called sebum. This can cause more pimples or acne.

**BACKACHE:** An ache in the lower back is common. Extremely severe pain may be a sign of something else. We'll chat a bit more about this later in the chapter.

**BLOATING:** Your belly might feel a little bit full and tight. Pants may fit a bit more snugly or feel uncomfortable. This feeling usually goes away after a few days.

**BREAST TENDERNESS:** Due to changes in hormones, your breasts may feel more swollen or lumpy and a bit uncomfortable.

**CRAMPS:** This is throbbing or cramping pains in the abdomen or lower belly region. Some people can have very uncomfortable cramps—sometimes they're just annoying.

**FATIGUE:** You may feel tired and have lower energy because of low estrogen levels. If you have really heavy periods, low iron from heavy bleeding could make you more tired.

**HEADACHE:** Headaches may happen because of the drop in estrogen before your period. These can last a few hours or days during your period.

# The Emotional Symptoms

We know that changes in hormones affect us physically, but they can also affect our emotions and brain. Symptoms include:

**DIFFICULTY FOCUSING:** Sometimes tension and anxiety make it harder to focus. You may experience "brain fog." This is where you don't feel like your mind is working clearly and there is a haze in your thoughts. You may have a hard time concentrating, memorizing, or making decisions. If you feel this way during school, be patient with yourself and your hormones. You're smart and capable, and sometimes it's just more difficult to focus because of changing hormones. Many people go through this!

**FEELING VULNERABLE:** A drop in estrogen and progesterone may cause you to feel vulnerable. Being vulnerable could mean some feelings of anxiety about being rejected, embarrassed, or judged.

**MOOD SWINGS:** Estrogen levels rise and fall throughout the menstrual cycle, which can cause mood swings. You may feel changes in your mood even if nothing in the outside world has changed. You may feel happy and then sad within a few minutes without any real reason. Sometimes you'll also feel really good and feel like you can focus even better than usual.

**TENSION OR ANXIETY:** Anxiety may cause you to worry about a lot of things or feel more nervous or tense. Tension can feel like emotional strain, where you can't think as clearly. These symptoms could be because of the sudden drop in estrogen and progesterone right before your period.

Just remember that if you are having any negative emotions, your mood can change—I'm here to remind you that you are strong and capable and amazing!

## JOURNALING

All of these emotional changes might feel really new, and you might not know exactly what to do about them. Something that can help you work through your emotions is journaling. You can use a guided journal with questions you can answer or just use a blank journal or notebook. Write about whatever you want—how you're feeling, what you're grateful for, what you did that day—there's no limit! Journaling is a special time and space for you to just sit and write about what you are thinking and feeling—it can also help you process some of the new emotions you're feeling. I journal every morning. When I am stressed, it helps me work through thoughts or emotions I have had that day or the day before. I love it! It's something you can do anywhere. For example, you can jot your thoughts down on a note or email app on your phone, in an old notebook that you can decorate, or on a scrap piece of paper. I've even journaled on a napkin!

# WHAT WILL MY PERIOD LOOK LIKE?

You may look at the amount of blood coming out during your period and think, *That's a lot!* But really, you only lose about 2 to 3 tablespoons of blood during your period. This can range a bit—it all depends whether you have heavy, regular, or light periods. If your periods are heavy, you may lose more blood and need to change your period products (like pads or tampons) often. Light periods are when you don't bleed quite as much. You may have heavy periods one month and light periods the next. The level in between is referred to as "regular."

With different flows, you may also see different colors of blood. The colors may change during your period or from cycle to cycle. You may see dark red blood or brown blood at the beginning or end of a period. Red means fresh blood and a steady flow. Pink blood can be at the beginning or end of your period as well. This may just be cervical fluid, which is clear, mixed with blood. You may see all of these colors or only a couple. It's all normal! Your blood may also be thick or thin. You may even see blood clots during your period. These are just small chunks of blood—that is your uterine lining shedding mixed with some blood, and that's normal, too. Clots can be a range of colors, from bright to dark red. Clots should usually be smaller than the size of a quarter.

# HOW LONG WILL MY PERIOD LAST?

The length of a period varies from person to person, so don't compare yourself to your friends. Every body is different. Your menstrual cycle starts on the first day that you bleed, or the first day of your period. That starts the "clock" on that menstrual cycle. On average, cycles last 21 to 35 days. That's the time between the start of two different periods. Periods may last anywhere from about two to seven days.

When you first get your period, you may have longer cycles. Cycle lengths may change from month to month as your body matures. The same is true with how long your period lasts. You may have longer or shorter periods the first couple of years. After that, your body will start to balance out, and you may have a shorter time between cycles and your period may last the same amount of days each cycle.

It's important to track your cycles because everyone is different and there are so many "normals." It's important to learn what is normal *for you*. If you start to track what your body does with your cycles, you'll know if you have an irregular period for you. But remember, for the first couple of years, your periods may be pretty unpredictable, and that's normal! Sometimes it can take five to seven years for things to balance out, so be patient with your body.

# WHEN SOMETHING FEELS DIFFERENT

You'll experience a lot of changes, and many of these are normal. If you know your body and what's going on inside, it will be easier to feel empowered and be less surprised by changes, but it'll also be easier to recognize when something isn't quite right. Knowledge is power! Now that you know what's normal, I will help walk you through some things that may be warning signs that something else is going on.

If you experience anything we discuss in this section, you may need to talk to a trusted adult or healthcare provider. Working with your doctor to reduce or eliminate these issues can help. If you think, *Whoa, that's me!* it never hurts to ask just to make sure. Whenever you have questions about your body and period, talk to a trusted adult. They have experience in this topic and can help you figure out if it's a normal change or something that requires a little more investigation.

**ENDOMETRIOSIS:** If you feel severe pain that makes you miss school or you can't do the activities and hobbies you usually love to do, this could be endometriosis. If you have crampy or sharp pain with defecation (pooping) when you are on your period, this could also be a sign of endometriosis. Endometriosis is when your endometrium, or the lining of the uterus, implants somewhere outside the uterus. It can be on

your ovaries, fallopian tubes, or somewhere else. It acts the same as the tissue inside your uterus, so it grows and then breaks down like it would during a period, but there is nowhere for this blood and tissue to go. This causes severe pain. You may have lower abdominal or pelvic pain (lower belly pain) that can start days before your period and then continue days into your period.

**PMDD:** We already chatted about PMS. Premenstrual dysphoric disorder (PMDD) is a more extreme version of PMS. You might have typical PMS symptoms like fatigue, bloating, and cramps, but with PMDD, you may have extreme mood swings that can affect your relationships with friends and family. These symptoms usually start 7 to 10 days before your period. In PMDD, you would feel one or more of the following:

- Sadness or hopelessness

- Overwhelming anxiety or tension

- Extreme moodiness, like being very irritable or angry

    These are similar to the emotional changes we talked about in PMS, but if they feel unmanageable or overwhelming and are affecting your days and relationships, it's best to ask a trusted adult or healthcare provider about what is going on.

**HEAVY PERIODS (MENORRHAGIA):** The flow of your period is important to pay attention to, but remember that for the first couple of years your periods may be irregular. You may have lighter or heavier periods before your body comes into balance, but if you have heavy periods, it's best to ask a trusted adult about the situation just to make sure. If you have multiple periods in a row where you bleed more than eight days in a row, need to change your period products every hour because they are getting soaked, or pass clots larger than a quarter, you may have menorrhagia. Heavy periods could suggest underlying causes that make you bleed more than normal, like fibroids or polyps, so talk to an adult.

**AMENORRHEA:** This is when you don't have periods. If you have already started menstruating and then you stop having periods for over 90 days, this is amenorrhea. If you haven't started your period by age 15 or 16 but your breasts have developed, it's best to talk to a healthcare provider about this, too. Amenorrhea can be caused by overexercising, not eating enough calories, or stress. Healthy periods are a sign of overall health. But remember, it's okay to have irregular or missed periods during the first year or two of having your period.

# CHAPTER 3

# LOVING MY PERIOD, LOVING ME

• • • • • • • • • • • • • • • • • • • • • • • • •

You are doing an amazing job. Thanks for coming this far with me on this journey of learning more about your body so you can feel powerful in making decisions that are best for you.

This chapter is all about taking care of, loving, and respecting your body. Part of appreciating what your body is able to do is realizing how incredible it is. We go through the complicated choreographed dance of periods every single month!

I've mentioned a couple of times that it is important to track your period. Tracking your period and symptoms can help you notice what is normal for you. Do you get a period every cycle? Is it heavy or light? Seeing patterns in your period can help you prepare for the next one and understand your body more. Appreciating and loving your body is so important as you move through life. You are strong and capable, and it's great to embrace yourself!

# TRACKING YOUR PERIOD

One of the best ways to learn about your body is to listen to it and track your cycle. This means noting when you get your period and any details about it. There are many different ways to track your menstrual cycles. You could use journals or apps. A great starting point is just to write down and track when your period starts and when it ends. This can help you see whether your cycle is regular (happening about every 28 days).

When you track your cycle, remember that your first day is the first day you bleed, and each cycle is usually around 28 days. The 28 days are the days between when you first start bleeding in one cycle to your first bleed in the next cycle. It's also important to know what your "normal" is so you can recognize when something is off and ask a trusted adult if you have concerns. We'll talk about this more in the next chapter. The timing is the most important thing to track.

Some people track when they ovulate, too. That's pretty much the midpoint between the start of two different cycles, about 14 days after the first day you start bleeding. You may see thicker cervical fluid, and it may become a little more white and less clear during this time.

Other great things to keep track of are the color and consistency of your period. Knowing the color of your period and how heavy or light it is from cycle to cycle can really help you understand your body. You may start to see patterns, especially after the first couple of years of menstruating, when your cycle starts to become more predictable. This can help you notice if something is off for a couple of cycles. For example, you may notice that your period starts off light but starts to get heavier from day to day or that you start to bleed more heavily from cycle to cycle or are experiencing more clots than usual.

A cool thing about tracking your period is that it helps you recognize and be able to explain what's going on. If you have a question or start experiencing symptoms that hint that something else could be going on, you can show your healthcare provider exactly how your menstrual cycles have been. All this information is super helpful to them.

If you start by tracking the timing of your period first, that's great. After you feel comfortable with that, you can start making notes of other things like:

- **The color of your blood:** Is it pink, red, dark red, or a different color? Does it change throughout your cycle?

- **The flow of your period:** Is it heavy, light, or spotting (which is very light bleeding)?

- **Any physical or emotional changes you feel during your period:** Are your breasts tender? How are you feeling? Are you having pain? Are you getting cramps? Have you had to miss any activities or school because of your symptoms? Are you craving any foods? How is your energy level? You can make note of when you notice those symptoms arrive and go away.

- **Things that help your symptoms:** Did a heating pad on your stomach help? What about exercising? If so, make a note of it! This way, you can remember what works for you during future cycles.

It can be fun getting to know your body through tracking your period. Don't overwhelm yourself with tracking too much at first, but as you get more comfortable, I hope you'll see how it can help you learn more about your body.

# TAKING CARE OF YOUR CHANGING BODY

You now know the facts, what to expect from your first period, and how to be in tune with your body, so let's chat about how to take care of your period and period hygiene. We'll go into detail about the range of period products available and the advantage of each, so you can make your own decisions about what's right for you.

In addition to period products, a few self-care tips can be helpful during your period. For example, since you may be more likely to get acne when your hormones are changing, washing your face in the morning and at night can prevent acne. Use gentle soaps and face products—fragrance-free products are best, but even just rinsing your face with water is great. And drinking plenty of water can help prevent symptoms like cramps.

These are just a couple of suggestions—in chapter 4, we'll dive deeper into healthy choices you can make, including the best foods for your mental and physical health. But first, let's check out the different period products available so you can be prepared and comfortable on your period.

# HOW DO I CHOOSE A PERIOD PRODUCT?

There are a lot of things to consider when choosing a period product. First off, you'll want to experiment a bit to find the most comfortable product for you. You don't want to feel the tampon all day, and maybe pads rub against your skin. Choose the product that is the most comfortable for you during your period so you can still do all the things you love while menstruating. You may even switch between products from day to day.

Besides comfort, there are other consideration when making a selection, such as the safety of the product. Some tampons and pads are scented. The chemicals in those products that make them scented could be harmful to your health, so choose fragrance-free products whenever you can.

Another thing to consider is the sustainability of period products. Things like reusable menstrual cups are a more environmentally friendly choice because then a bunch of products aren't thrown away (or bought) each month. They're friendly to your wallet *and* the planet! These may be expensive up front, but if you can afford them, they can help save money over time because you won't have to buy new products every single month. If period products are not affordable for you or your family, many groups are making period products more accessible. See "Access for All" on page 49 for more on this.

# POPULAR PERIOD PRODUCTS

There's a whole aisle at the supermarket with pads, tampons, pantyliners—and for daytime, nighttime, heavy days, and so on. I get so many questions about period products, and I'll answer them in this section.

Period products are what you use to collect or soak up period blood so it doesn't get on your clothes. The big thing to remember is that you may need to try a couple of products to find the ones you like and feel most comfortable with.

I've changed what I've used throughout the years, and the ones I currently use depend on what I'm doing. For example, if you play sports, you may wear something different compared to when you are sleeping. For example, pads can be impractical when swimming because they soak up water and get heavy and lumpy. Your friends may love tampons, and you may prefer pads. That's totally fine—we're all different! You can ask a trusted adult or friend for their advice, too.

Even with products, it's totally normal to get a little blood on your underwear or pants. This happens to many of us. I've definitely experienced this. It's nothing to worry about. The blood usually comes out with soap and cold water.

Whether you use pads or tampons, it's important to avoid scented products—they can cause infections. It's normal to have some smell during your period. If your period has a very overwhelming smell, it could signal an infection, so talk to a health professional. They can prescribe medication to help clear it up.

Change pads and tampons as often as necessary, but don't wait more than eight hours. This is especially true for tampons. A tampon that stays in too long can cause a fairly severe infection and reaction. If your products are getting soaked through every hour or so, that's considered heavy bleeding, so talk to a trusted adult.

## Pads

Pads are a product you put in your underwear. They usually have an absorbent side (the pad) and a sticky side that adheres to the inside of your underwear. Most options are disposable (used once and then thrown away), but there are also some reusable pads. Reusable pads may have elastic or snaps in the back that attach to your underwear.

Change your pad every few hours or when it's soaked with blood. When replacing a disposable pad, wrap it up in the next pad's wrapping or toilet paper and throw it in the trash. Be sure not to flush wrappers or pads down the toilet. If you've ever seen the sign "Don't flush feminine products down the toilet," it is talking about period products.

Pads come in many different forms. You can choose your pad based on your flow. There are super, slender, overnight, maxi, mini, regular, and thin. Some have "wings" that wrap around the bottom of the underwear to secure them in place. Pantyliners can be used when you're not bleeding that much. Maxi, overnight, and super pads can be used for heavier bleeding.

## Tampons

Tampons come in different sizes, like light, regular, and super, depending on how much blood they can absorb. I recommend starting with the smallest size and seeing if it lasts you a few hours. If you have to change it every hour or two, go up a size. You want to use the lightest or smallest size that can last you a few hours. Too big a tampon could be uncomfortable.

Some tampons are packaged in applicators, which is the plastic or cardboard around the cottony tampon. The applicator is only there to make it easier to insert the tampon—it gets thrown out after the tampon goes in. If the tampon doesn't have an applicator, just use your finger to push it in.

### Here's how to insert a tampon:

1. Wash your hands.

2. Get into a comfortable position, like sitting on the toilet with your knees spread apart to relax the muscles around your vagina. The tampon is much more comfortable to insert when you're relaxed.

3. Unwrap the tampon and gently push it into your vagina with the applicator or your finger. Push it in at a slight diagonal angle toward your back rather than straight up. You shouldn't feel too

much resistance; you may have to change the angle slightly until you find a comfortable fit. If you have difficulty, ask a trusted adult who has used tampons to show you how you would insert it. The tampon should be fully inside you, with the string hanging out.

4. Discard the wrapper and the applicator in the trash, not the toilet.

5. Make sure the tampon is comfortable. Having a tampon in should not hurt. If it hurts or you can feel it, you may not have pushed the tampon in far enough. You should pretty much forget it's there. Again, don't worry if you don't get the insertion right on the first try. It may take a couple of times to insert it comfortably.

6. To take out the tampon, sit on the toilet with your knees apart, and slowly pull on the string. Remember to stay relaxed. It's easier to remove a tampon when it is soaked or wet from absorbing blood. (In fact, don't wear tampons when you are not on your period.) Wrap the used tampon in toilet paper and throw it in the garbage.

It's best to change out a tampon every four to eight hours or when it becomes soaked, and remember not to leave it in longer than eight hours. You may want to try different types to find what is most comfortable for you.

# Period Underwear

Period underwear look like regular underwear but have extra layers of material in them to soak up period blood. Some period underwear are disposable, and some are washable and reusable (making them environmentally friendly). Nowadays, some kinds of period underwear can hold as much blood as a couple of tampons. While these panties can seem more expensive than disposable period products, the reusable nature of them makes them more affordable in the long run.

# Menstrual Cups

Menstrual products are a great option because you only have to buy them once every couple of years so you create less waste and save money in the long run. Imagine the difference a choice like this will make for the planet! There are many different kinds, and they come with instructions on how to use them. Some are disposable, but most are reusable. The cup may seem kind of big, but you usually shouldn't feel it once it's in place. You may need a bit of practice inserting one to get it right. If you use a reusable menstrual cup, you'll remove and wash it about every 10 to 12 hours with fragrance-free and oil-free soap. For further instructions on care and use, check the product instructions that come with your particular menstrual cup.

## ACCESS FOR ALL

It's great that there are so many period product options, but not everyone has access to these products or education about them. Lack of access to period products can be another stressful event. If you get your period and have to worry about whether you can get products or if you'll bleed through your clothes, it can be really hard to focus on schoolwork or other activities. In recent years, people have banded together to help address this issue called "period poverty" in this country and around the globe. To learn more or to join the fight for access for all, check out organizations like Period.org, Freedom4Girls.co.uk, DignityPeriod.org, AllianceForPeriodSupplies.org, and #HappyPeriod.

# CHAPTER 4

# LIVING MY BEST PERIOD-POSITIVE LIFE

. . . . . . . . . . . . . . . . . . . . . . . .

Give yourself a pat on the back for all you've learned! We're going to keep building on the knowledge you have so you can move through your period with strength and grace. In this chapter, you will learn how to be your healthiest self. This health advice isn't just for your physical health; it's important for your mental health as well.

We'll chat about great things to eat to fuel yourself up so you can do all the activities you love. I'll give you advice on how to treat some PMS symptoms. You'll also learn how you can care for your mental health and what loving yourself means and looks like.

# EATING WELL

This is one of my favorite things to talk about: *food!*
What we eat can really impact how we feel every day.
The food choices we make can affect how we feel mentally, like how happy or patient we are, how well we can
focus, and how our period feels.

PMS symptoms are common. If you take steps to
care for your overall wellness, some of these symptoms will improve or may even go away. Talk about
feeling powerful! The healthier the food you put into
your body, the healthier your period will be. The
food you eat can actually send instructions to the
rest of your body.

You may start to hear about a lot of different diets,
but we're not talking about a diet to lose weight here.
We're talking about a lifestyle to be the best and
healthiest version of yourself.

There are a few important things to remember when
you eat, but there's no one-size-fits-all approach. We
all come from different cultural backgrounds, and we
have different likes and dislikes when it comes to food.
Plus, everyone responds differently to foods. The most
important point is that the more *whole* foods you eat
(meaning foods that came right off the tree or bush or
from the ground), the better. This means an apple is a
better choice than apple juice and a potato is better for
you than French fries.

If possible, it's also best to avoid sugars and pro-cessed foods. About 70 percent of packaged foods in the grocery store have added sugar, and sugar can make period symptoms much worse. A general rule of thumb is that anything packaged is processed. To tell what's in a packaged food, look at the ingredients list. If there are more than five ingredients, the food item is usually processed. Avoiding sugary and processed foods can help prevent or reduce symptoms of PMS.

Here are some foods that can help you have an awesome, potentially pain-free period. While you might not be able to make selections from the following list at every meal, keeping these foods in mind will allow you to make healthy choices when you can.

## Leafy Greens

These include kale, spinach, arugula, lettuce, chard, and collard greens. Why are these good? When you bleed during your period, you lose iron. Leafy greens can help replace the iron you lose, which helps with energy. They can also lower the pain of cramps.

## Cruciferous Veggies

Broccoli, Brussels sprouts, and cauliflower have been found to lower symptoms of PMS.

## Dark Chocolate

Dark chocolate has magnesium in it. People with low magnesium can have worse PMS symptoms. The best choice is 70 percent or more cacao. My favorite is 88 percent dark chocolate.

## Berries

Berries like blueberries and strawberries have nutrients and antioxidants that can help protect your brain and regulate your mood.

# Other Whole Fruit

A serving of fruits like watermelon or oranges can help with symptoms of dysmenorrhea (painful bleeding).

# Proteins

Proteins like eggs, beef, chicken, tofu, and beans can help prevent you from craving certain foods on your period and can help make you feel satisfied. Red meat like steak can also help replace iron lost during your period. Eggs contain calcium and some magnesium and can help ease some pain during periods. Greek yogurt can be a great source of protein if you aren't sensitive to dairy, but some people have a tough time digesting the sugar (lactose) found in dairy products.

# Beans

Beans like black beans, chickpeas, kidney beans, and lentils are a great source of protein and fiber that can help you feel full and lower food cravings.

# Fish

The omega-3 fatty acids in fish like salmon, sardines, anchovies, and herring can help reduce pain and depressive symptoms.

## Fats

There are good and bad fats. Bad fats include trans fats, which are found in things like baked goods, fried foods, and frozen pizza (yes, processed foods!). Good fats are found in avocado, raw nuts, flaxseed, eggs, and animal meat.

## Turmeric

This is a delicious yellow spice that can help lower the symptoms of PMS, especially mood, behavioral, and physical symptoms. It can be sprinkled into soups and smoothies, over rice, into roasted veggies—get creative and give it a try!

## Nuts

Nuts are a good source of protein and healthy fat. There are important nutrients like magnesium in nuts such as pistachios, Brazil nuts, cashews, and almonds, which can help prevent PMS symptoms.

## High-Fiber Foods

High-fiber whole foods include choices like avocado, artichokes, apples, popcorn, brown rice, lentils, and kidney beans. These foods can help soak up and get rid of some chemicals that cause pain during your period.

# FAD DIETS

Many popular diets come and go. Don't let the trends on social media trick you! Fad diets usually don't work, or else they would stick around longer, right? Many people focus on calories or weight on the scale, but food is much more than that. Food is information for your body. A variety of healthy food is important for keeping you physically and mentally healthy. It keeps every part of your body working. The main ideas to focus on are *healthy* and *unprocessed*. Think of this as any food that doesn't have a label or that looks pretty much like it does in nature. It's important to celebrate our food—it keeps us thriving, and meals can bring families and people together, too. This social connection can lead us to be our happiest, healthiest selves as well!

# FEELING GREAT

In this section, I'll explain how to lower the negative symptoms that can come with periods, like cramps and headaches. Feeling great isn't just about getting rid of these symptoms once they happen—it's also doing things like yoga or exercise to prevent these things from happening in the first place. Here are some tips and tricks to tackle common symptoms and help you feel awesome during your period.

**CRAMPS:** Try using a heating pad or taking a warm bath. Massage can also help. Sometimes cramps can get worse if you are dehydrated, so drink plenty of water. Some foods mentioned earlier—leafy greens, nuts, fish, and turmeric—are anti-inflammatory, which can reduce cramps. On the other end, processed and sugary foods can make cramps worse. Try the tricks mentioned here before trying any medication.

There are some pain-relieving pills that you can take without a prescription, including ibuprofen and other anti-inflammatory medications. These medications can be dangerous at high levels, so make sure a caregiver and healthcare provider works with you to choose the right medication and explain exactly how and when to take it. It's best to take medication once the cramps have actually started, not to prevent the cramps.

**HEADACHES:** For headaches, try a cold compress on your forehead. Relaxation methods like meditating or yoga can help. And sleep! Sleep is always important and can help with many period symptoms. Getting enough water is also helpful.

Exercising during your period can really help you feel better. Exercise makes the body release endorphins, which are feel-good chemicals that also lower pain. Even light exercise like jogging, walking, swimming, biking, and dancing can really help lower pain and boost your mood. And sleeping 8 to 12 hours a night is important for your overall health, especially during your period so you can help avoid some PMS symptoms. Sleeping a lot isn't being lazy—when you're tired, it's your body telling you that you need rest!

# LOVING YOURSELF

Loving yourself is really taking time and space to take care of you—this includes your mental *and* physical health. It's also about having positive and helpful self-talk and a kind self-image. Let's explore some ways to make this happen.

## Self-Kindness

Think about this: Some people are nicer to their friends than they are to themselves. Try talking to yourself like you are your own best friend. If your friend didn't do well on a test, you would tell them, "It's okay—you are smart and capable and will do great next time!" Use this same positivity with yourself!

# Trading Your Screen for Real Life

FOMO (fear of missing out) is a big issue for teens, especially with social media. Take breaks from social media and screens—doing so is good for your mental health! Use this time to go for walks or hang out with friends in person. Going out in nature is a great way to show self-care. Spend 10 minutes counting birds at your local park or walking under trees down your street. Being in nature lowers stress and anxiety, helps with focus and test scores, and boosts immune cells that actually help fight off cancers!

# Taking Time to Reflect

Life gets busy and sometimes overwhelming. It's totally fine to say no to plans if you need some time for yourself. There will be a get-together another time!

One of the best things we can learn how to do is to listen to our body and our thoughts. One way to do this is to practice mindfulness or meditate.

Mindfulness is being aware of your thoughts and emotions in that moment. We can get caught up thinking about the past or future, but it's so important to celebrate the here and now. Mindfulness is paying attention: *How does the wind feel on your face? Can you notice the feeling of your feet on the ground? What does that strawberry taste like?* It's the opposite of autopilot.

Meditation is freeing or separating yourself from your thoughts. It lets you hang out with yourself and look at your thoughts without judging them. This can help you relax and make you more aware of what you are thinking.

**To start meditating:**

1. Sit in a quiet spot where you won't be interrupted.

2. Start with a few deep breaths.

3. Just breathe and let your thoughts float in and out of your mind without any judgment about them.

4. You can also focus on your breath, thinking "in" as you inhale and "out" as you exhale. This helps clear your mind of negative or stressful thoughts.

As I mentioned in a previous chapter, journaling is another way to get in tune with your body and yourself. Grab a notepad and pen and write about your day or whatever you're feeling. If you're in tune with your body and mind, you'll know what you need—like whether you will be happier taking a nap or going for a run. Part of loving yourself and your body is doing what is right for you at that time, and only *you* know what that means.

## TREAT YOURSELF: MY PERIOD PACK

Periods can be unpredictable, especially during the first two years. What's the best way to reduce worry about your period sneaking up on you when you aren't ready? Have a "period pack" containing all the essentials in your backpack or purse. Fill your period pack with your favorite period products, an extra pair of underwear, and travel-size wipes. If you know you get painful cramps or headaches on your period, it may be helpful to bring along some over-the-counter pain relievers—before you do this, talk to a medical professional and ask your parent or caregiver for permission.

# CHAPTER 5

# CELEBRATING MY SUPER PERIOD POWER!

You are amazing! Thank you for coming on this journey with me and learning more about yourself and your period. It's time to celebrate you, your periods, and a healthy life. I hope you appreciate and love your body and the amazing things it does. With all this knowledge, you now have what I call your super period power. Seriously, with this power, you'll be ready for what your body throws at you during menstruation. Your knowledge will help you handle it with confidence and strength. You now know what you can expect from your first period and how to navigate this big change in your life. You even know what is going on inside you every month that causes your period. No more mysteries!

# COMMUNITY AND SUPPORT

Even though you have this super period power, you may still have some questions. There may be situations that come up when you won't know exactly what is going on. This is expected and normal. Stay curious and ask questions of people you trust. Learning is always happening in any subject that you are studying. Even experts still learn something new every single day! Period challenges shouldn't and don't need to be handled alone. It's helpful and healthy to have a few friends or adults with whom you can discuss your questions and share some of the experiences you are facing.

You may be a support system for one of your friends, too! Having this group of people you know you can trust can help lower any anxiety around periods. You know they will have your back, and if you have any questions or concerns, you can turn to them.

I like to advise people on limiting their time on social media (even though I run a social media page!). It's easy to get sucked into social media and miss what's going on in the real world. And some of what's online can be very negative.

I do love social media for a few things, though. Some accounts are very positive and educational. One piece of advice I give is to choose people you follow very carefully—only choose accounts that teach you something and make you feel good about yourself.

There are some great accounts you can follow that give puberty and period advice, like ours: @MedicineExplained. These kinds of accounts can be part of your community and help you continue learning about your health and body.

As you continue to grow, you'll find people who have gone through the same things you are going through. It can feel super comforting to hear, "You've gone through that, too!?" When we talk openly about our periods with trusted people, we can share our experiences with one another and not feel so alone in the journey. Talking about your experiences and learning from others what you can expect helps lower some fear and anxiety about periods. And it can help you feel less alone.

We need more people talking about periods and their experiences so there is less anxiety and stigma around the topic. Menstruation is a natural process—and shouldn't be a taboo topic. The more we feel confident talking about our experiences, the more we will help empower others with real knowledge about periods. Conversations help us develop an awareness about how varied experiences can be. The more we share and listen, the more we can learn and help one another have our happiest and healthiest periods and lives.

## KEEP SLEEP IN MIND!

Sleep is super important to health, but did you know it can even affect what foods you crave? Even just one night of bad sleep changes the way your body handles sugar. Sleeping helps clean out your brain. Your brain builds up toxins and waste products as the day goes on, and when you sleep, your brain cells spread out a bit, creating a space between them to wash out the junk.

Getting good sleep helps protect your mental health and immune system. Sleeping well can help you participate in sports, theater, art, or schoolwork to the best of your abilities. Good sleep helps you grow and will help you have healthy periods.

How much sleep is enough sleep? Well, people between the ages of 6 and 12 should sleep between 9 and 12 hours a night. Anyone between the ages of 13 and 18 should sleep 8 to 10 hours a night. We can't "catch up" on sleep—we really need a steady pattern. It's central to helping us thrive and the key to having a happy and healthy period and life.

# CONCLUSION

Congrats! You've made it to the end of this book! Even though this book is coming to a close, you're only at the beginning of your period journey. You will continue to learn more and more as you go along and have your own period experiences. This book is a guideline that you can keep coming back to in order to know what to expect and to reference all that you've taken in on anatomy, nutrition, and tips for being the best you. Knowledge is power! You will continue to learn new things constantly. After some experience and time with menstruating, you are going to understand even more about your unique body and how to take care of yourself and your periods.

You are awesome and have so much greatness ahead of you in your life, and your period will be a part of you during your life journey for the next few decades. It's great that you've started off on the right foot, knowing how to best deal with it so every month is the best it can be. Now that you know what to expect, I hope you will feel stronger and more capable navigating these times. Celebrate your period! It's amazing what your body can do, and with this knowledge, you're better equipped to move through the world with confidence. Period power!

# GLOSSARY

‖‖‖‖‖‖‖‖‖‖‖‖‖‖‖‖‖‖‖‖‖‖‖‖‖‖‖‖‖‖‖‖

(For additional definitions, see pages 8 to 11.)

**CERVICAL FLUID:** Also called "vaginal fluid" or "discharge," this is fluid and mucus created by an increase in hormones

**CERVIX (SUR·VUHKS):** The narrow opening at the end of the uterus that connects to the vagina

**DYSMENORRHEA (DUH·SMEH·NR·EE·UH):** Pain during a period, which can be from cramping

**ENDOMETRIUM (EN·DOW·MEE·TREE·UHM):** The lining of the uterus that is shed during a period

**FEMALE GENITALS:** The area of the body comprised of the vulva, which includes the opening of the vagina, the labia majora and minora, and the clitoris, as well as internal genitalia

**GENETICS:** The study of heredity, or characteristics of the body that pass down through generations

**HORMONES:** Chemicals in the body that initiate puberty and control the menstrual cycle

**HUMAN ANATOMY:** The structure of the human body

**HUMAN PHYSIOLOGY (FI·ZEE·AA·LUH·JEE):** The way the structures (anatomy) of the body work

**MENARCHE (MUH·-NAAR·KEE):** A first period

**MENSTRUAL CUP:** A small, bowl-like structure inserted into the vagina to collect menstrual blood

**MENSTRUAL CYCLE:** A four-stage cycle that begins on the first day of your period and lasts about 28 days

**OVA:** Eggs or the unfertilized cells stored in the ovaries

**OVARIES (OW·VR·EEZ):** Two small organs that store your eggs and release one each month, and release hormones

**PADS:** Narrow strips of absorbent material that stick to underwear to collect menstrual blood

**PERIOD:** Also called menstruation, this is the bleeding phase of the menstrual cycle

**PERIOD TRACKER:** An app used to record the date and details of a period

**PERIOD UNDERWEAR:** Underwear specifically made with extra material to absorb menstrual blood

**PREMENSTRUAL SYNDROME (PMS):** Physical and emotional changes before a period caused by hormones

**PRIMARY AMENORRHEA (AY·MEH·NR·EE·UH):** When a first period has not occurred by the age of 15

**SECONDARY AMENORRHEA (*AY·MEH·NR·EE·UH*):** When a woman stops menstruating for three months or more after regular periods

**SECONDARY SEX CHARACTERISTICS:** Changes in the body that signal puberty

**SPOTTING:** Very light bleeding

**TAMPON:** A plug-shaped product made of absorbent material that is inserted into the vagina to absorb menstrual blood

**UTERUS (*YOO·TR·UHS*):** The organ where the endometrium develops; also called the womb

**VAGINA:** The opening and canal that connects the uterus and cervix with the vulva

# RESOURCES

Here are some select additional resources on puberty and well-being. There is a lot of information online, so make sure the sites you visit are written by experts. For any concerns, I recommend first chatting with a health-care provider or a trusted adult.

## Books

*Celebrate Your Body* by Sonya Renee Taylor

*Celebrate Your Body 2* by Dr. Lisa Klein and Dr. Carrie Leff

*Celebrate Your Feelings* by Lauren Rivers

*Mindfulness for Kids in 10 Minutes a Day* by Mayra Bradley

*Self-Love Journal for Teen Girls* by Cindy Whitehead

# Websites

### American College of Obstetricians and Gynecologists (ACOG)

This web page from the ACOG offers tons of information on changes in the body during puberty.
ACOG.org/womens-health/faqs/your-changing-body-puberty-in-girls

### Body Positivity

This website reminds readers to focus on loving the body they're in.
BodyPositive.com

### Center for Humane Technology

The youth tool kit on this site offers insights about how social media works.
HumaneTech.com/youth

### KidsHealth

This web page contains doctor-reviewed information about puberty.
KidsHealth.org/en/kids/puberty.html

### The Menstrual Health Hub

This website offers resources on menstrual health around the world, as well as a "Menstrual Memo" providing updates and news for subscribers.
MHhub.org

**National Health Services**

This site, from England's nationally funded healthcare system, discusses the changes that occur during puberty.
NHS.uk/live-well/sexual-health/stages-of-puberty-what-happens-to-boys-and-girls

**National Institute of Environmental Health Sciences**

This site offers information, games, and activities on an array of health topics from nutrition to the environment.
Kids.NIEHS.NIH.gov/topics/healthy-living/index.htm

**Office on Women's Health**

This site from the U.S. Department of Health and Human Services offers comprehensive information on all aspects of menstruation.
WomensHealth.gov/menstrual-cycle

**Peach, Lucy. "The Power of the Period."**

TED Talk, 2017. This video offers an empowering perspective on the menstrual cycle.
TED.com/talks/lucy_peach_the_power_of_the_period

**Planned Parenthood**

This web page contains an overview on the basics of puberty as well as answers to some common questions.
PlannedParenthood.org/learn/teens/puberty

**U.S. Department of Agriculture**

This website contains lots of teen-specific nutrition information.
Nutrition.gov/topics/nutrition-age/teens

# REFERENCES

The American College of Obstetricians and Gynecologists. "Amenorrhea: Absence of Periods." Last modified October 2020. ACOG.org/womens-health/faqs /amenorrhea-absence-of-periods.

The American College of Obstetricians and Gynecologists. "Heavy Menstrual Bleeding." Last modified May 2021. ACOG.org/womens-health/faqs/heavy -menstrual-bleeding.

The American College of Obstetricians and Gynecologists. "Premenstrual Syndrome (PMS)." Last modified May 2021. ACOG.org/womens-health/faqs/premenstrual -syndrome.

The American College of Obstetricians and Gynecologists. "Your First Period." Last modified February 2019. ACOG.org/womens-health/faqs/your-first-period.

Babakhani, Khatereh, Gity Sotoudeh, Fereydoun Siassi, and Mostafa Qorbani. "Comparison of Vegetable Intake in Nurses with and without Premenstrual Syndrome:

A Case-Control Study." *Shiraz E-Medical Journal* 21, no. 2 (2020): e91319. doi.org/10.5812/semj.91319.

Centers for Disease Control and Prevention. "Heavy Menstrual Bleeding." Last modified December 2017. CDC .gov/ncbddd/blooddisorders/women/menorrhagia.html.

Johns Hopkins Medicine. "Premenstrual Dysphoric Disorder (PMDD)." Accessed November 4, 2021. HopkinsMedicine.org/health/conditions-and-diseases /premenstrual-dysphoric-disorder-pmdd.

Mayo Clinic. "Endometriosis." Last modified July 24, 2018. MayoClinic.org/diseases-conditions/endometriosis /symptoms-causes/syc-20354656.

McDowell, Margaret A., Debra J. Brody, and Jeffery P. Hughes. "Has Age at Menarche Changed? Results from the National Health and Nutrition Examination Survey (NHANES) 1999–2004." *Journal of Adolescent Health* 40, no. 3 (2007): 227–31. doi:10.1016/j.jadohealth .2006.10.002.

National Health Services. "Heavy Periods." Last modified November 2021. NHS.uk/conditions/heavy-periods.

National Health Services. "Stages of Puberty: What Happens to Boys and Girls." Last modified November 16, 2018. NHS.uk/live-well/sexual-health/stages-of-puberty -what-happens-to-boys-and-girls.

Office on Women's Health. "Your Menstrual Cycle." Last modified March 16, 2018. WomensHealth.gov/menstrual -cycle/your-menstrual-cycle.

Planned Parenthood. "How Do I Use Tampons, Pads, Period Underwear, and Menstrual Cups?" Accessed November 4, 2021. PlannedParenthood.org/learn /health-and-wellness/menstruation/how-do-i-use -tampons-pads-and-menstrual-cups.

Planned Parenthood. "Menstruation." Accessed November 4, 2021. PlannedParenthood.org/learn /health-and-wellness/menstruation.

Saeedian Kia, Afsaneh, Reza Amani, and Bahman Cheraghian. "The Association between the Risk of Premenstrual Syndrome and Vitamin D, Calcium, and Magnesium Status among University Students: A Case Control Study." *Health Promotion Perspectives* 5, no. 3 (2015): 225–30. doi.org/10.15171/hpp.2015.027.

Sanger-Katz, Margot. "You'd Be Surprised at How Many Foods Contain Added Sugar." *The New York Times.* May 21, 2016. NYTimes.com/2016/05/22/upshot /it-isnt-easy-to-figure-out-which-foods-contain- sugar.html.

# INDEX

# Acknowledgments

I'd like to thank the support of my family, my partner, and the team who made this book possible. Also, I want to thank the Medicine Explained community and the beautiful people who are curious about their changing bodies and are reading this book!

# About the Author

**AMANDA D'ALMEIDA** is a fourth-year MD/MPH candidate in New Orleans, Louisiana. She is planning on going into a family medicine program. She is CEO and cofounder of Medicine Explained, a 501(3)(c) organization and health education platform aimed to empower people with health information. Medicine Explained has more than 1.8 million followers on social media. She also co-hosts the podcast *The Nuance*. Amanda is passionate about social, environmental, and lifestyle interventions to support health. She is involved in local groups and national policy changes to address the intersection of human and environmental health.